C000244798

THE LAST DAYS OF STEAM IN
PLYMOUTH AND CORNWALL

To the footplate crews and shed staff who operated in the area covered in this book, GWR, SR, BRWR and BRSR, and to the 'Grange' class loco, R.I.P.

THE LAST DAYS OF STEAM IN
PLYMOUTH AND CORNWALL

—MAURICE DART—

ALAN SUTTON

First published in the United Kingdom in 1990 by
Alan Sutton Publishing Ltd · Phoenix Mill · Stroud · Gloucestershire

First published in the United States of America in 1991 by
Alan Sutton Publishing Inc. · Wolfeboro Falls · NH 03896–0848

Copyright © Maurice Dart 1990

All rights reserved. No part of this publication may be reproduced, stored in a retrieval system, or transmitted, in any form or by any means, electronic, mechanical, photocopying, recording or otherwise, without the prior permission of the publishers and copyright holders.

British Library Cataloguing in Publication Data
Dart, Maurice
The last days of steam in Plymouth and Cornwall.
1. Devon. Plymouth. Steam locomotives, history
2. Cornwall. Railway services : Great Western Railway.
Steam locomotives, history
I. Title
625.2610942358

ISBN 0-86299-810-7

Library of Congress Cataloging in Publication Data applied for

Endpapers: Front: At Newquay on 26.7.58 waiting to depart is Laira's 'Modified Hall' class 4–6–0 7909 'Heveningham Hall' on a through working to Plymouth North Road.

Terry Nicholls

Back: A pair of Penzance-allocated 4500 class 2–6–2Ts at Lelant with a train from St Ives to St Erth on 14.7.61. The rear engine is 4566, the front one being 4549, with a GWR-type buffer beam number and still retaining inside steam pipes.

Peter Gray

Typeset in Palatino 9/10
Typesetting and origination by
Alan Sutton Publishing Limited
Printed in Great Britain by
Camelot Press, Trowbridge, Wiltshire.

Introduction

Journeying westwards by either Great Western Railway or Southern Railway routes one was never afraid of being caught asleep at Plymouth, as on the GWR route the descent of Hemerdon bank, with brake applications after the mid point, and on the SR route the downhill curving run from Shillamill tunnel, with the rumble and vibration when crossing the Tavy viaduct, were sure to make one stir from deepest slumbers. Hemerdon is still with us, although less dramatic, and the SR route is reduced to branch line status from Bere Alston only. This, to me, typifies the entry to the area covered by this book.

Plymouth's suburban services and branch lines have all but disappeared with station and route closures; the 'Saltash Motors' are a memory of the past. No longer do double-headed express trains slog up Hemerdon, and on the SR the memory of 'The Brighton' is becoming dim. The magic of the roundhouse at Laira has past, although there is a diesel maintenance depot there, and perhaps the ghost of a B4 tank haunts the warehouse on the site of Friary shed.

Once past Laira the banks become frequent, and called for a special breed of footplate crew to handle the engines with heavy trains, braking on the downgrades and standing starts to the climbs, such as out of Par on the main line west. The GW Cornish main line abounds in sharp curves in addition to heavy gradients, and the branch lines presented even more fearsome problems with gradients of 1:40 commonplace. Many branches have been closed, together with some main-line stations. The SR route passed through more isolated districts with, in some cases, the station and village or town being a considerable distance apart. The sparse service on the fingers of the Withered Arm fell victim to Beeching's ruthless pruning, although small portions are coming to life again at Launceston and possibly in the distant future even Wenford. A small section in Cornwall, from Calstock to Gunnislake, retains a passenger service.

The Southern was virtually annihilated overnight in Cornwall, and again the magic of the Beattie Well tanks at Wadebridge, a T9 on the turntable at Padstow and Ns and T9s simmering away at Bude are but memories.

Examples of many of the loco types which worked the area have been preserved, but sadly no 'Grange' was saved. These, together with 'Halls' and 'Moguls', were the workhorses of the GWR main line to Penzance. Apparently it was quite an experience to hit the curve leading onto Moorswater viaduct on an 'Up' train on the footplate of a 'Mogul'! Another nightmare for footplate crews was Pinnock tunnel – 1173 yds long and full of bends on a 1:50 incline against the load – referred to by St Blazey drivers as 'The nearest place to hell you could get in Cornwall'.

By 1958 the diesels had started to appear on the main line and branches, and steam began to disappear. Working conditions on the diesel locos, HSTs and DMUs are better and less arduous than on steam locos with, for example, no more cab tarpaulins. What was fun, exhilaration and manna to the railway enthusiast was hard graft for the railwaymen.

Even though large tracts of Cornwall are now without a railway, that which survives presents a better, faster service than years ago, and further improvements with a route diversion are to come. In the Plymouth area the line between Bere Alston and Tavistock and possibly even to Meldon may re-open, to give a diversionary route for use when weather problems are encountered in the Dawlish area.

This book depicts the days when steam reigned supreme in this area and all routes and branch lines were operating, together with a few industrial lines. I hope it awakens fond memories.

Maurice Dart

Acknowledgements

I would like to thank the following for supplying additional photographs to my own and/or giving consent to use them in this book: Colin Henry Bastin, Anthony Bennett, Harry Cowan, Larry Crosier, Mike Daly, the late Edward Dart, Tony Fairclough for the late Brian A. Butt, Peter Gray, George Hemmett, Lens of Sutton, Michael Mensing, Michael Messenger, Terry Nicholls, Denis Richards, Roy Taylor, Roger Winnen and Revd Peter Witney. Also, Larry Crosier, George Hemmett and Edgar Whitear for information over the years; Mike Blake for drawing the map; Kevin Robertson for presenting the idea of this book to me, and education in procedure; John Vaughan for advice over the choice of photographs; Emily Hancock for tolerance, encouragement and the use of her dining-room while preparing the book; Walter Julian for checking the proof copy with me; and Joan Kendall for typing the manuscript, after deciphering my writing.

Reference Sources

Southern Railway Time Tables 1947 onwards.
British Railways Western Region Working Time Tables 1951/1958.
Track Layout Diagrams of the GWR and BRWR Sections 10/11/12/13/14 – R.A. Cooke.
Track Layout Diagrams of the Southern Railway and BRSR Section 6 – G.A. Pryer.
Itineries for the Ark Royal and Cornish Clayliner Railtours – Branch Line Society.
Locomotives of the Great Western Railway Parts 5/8/9 – Railway Correspondence and Travel Society.
The Withered Arm – T.W.E. Roche and Peter Semmens.
Locomotive Stock Book 1952 – Railway Correspondence and Travel Society.
Locomotive Stock Alterations 1952/1954 – Railway Correspondence and Travel Society.
A Regional History of the Railways of Great Britain, Volume l, The West Country – David St John Thomas.
The Tavistock, Launceston and Princetown Railways – G. H. Anthony.
G.W.R. Locomotive Allocations, First and Last Sheds 1922–1967 – J.W.P. Rowledge.
Industrial Locomotives Handbook 7EL 1987 – Industrial Railway Society.
Industrial Locomotives of South Western England, Handbook H 1977 – Industrial Railway Society.
The Devonport Dockyard Story – Lt. Cdr. K.V. Burns DSM RN.
My personal record books since 1947 of locomotive sightings, photography and locomotive allocations.

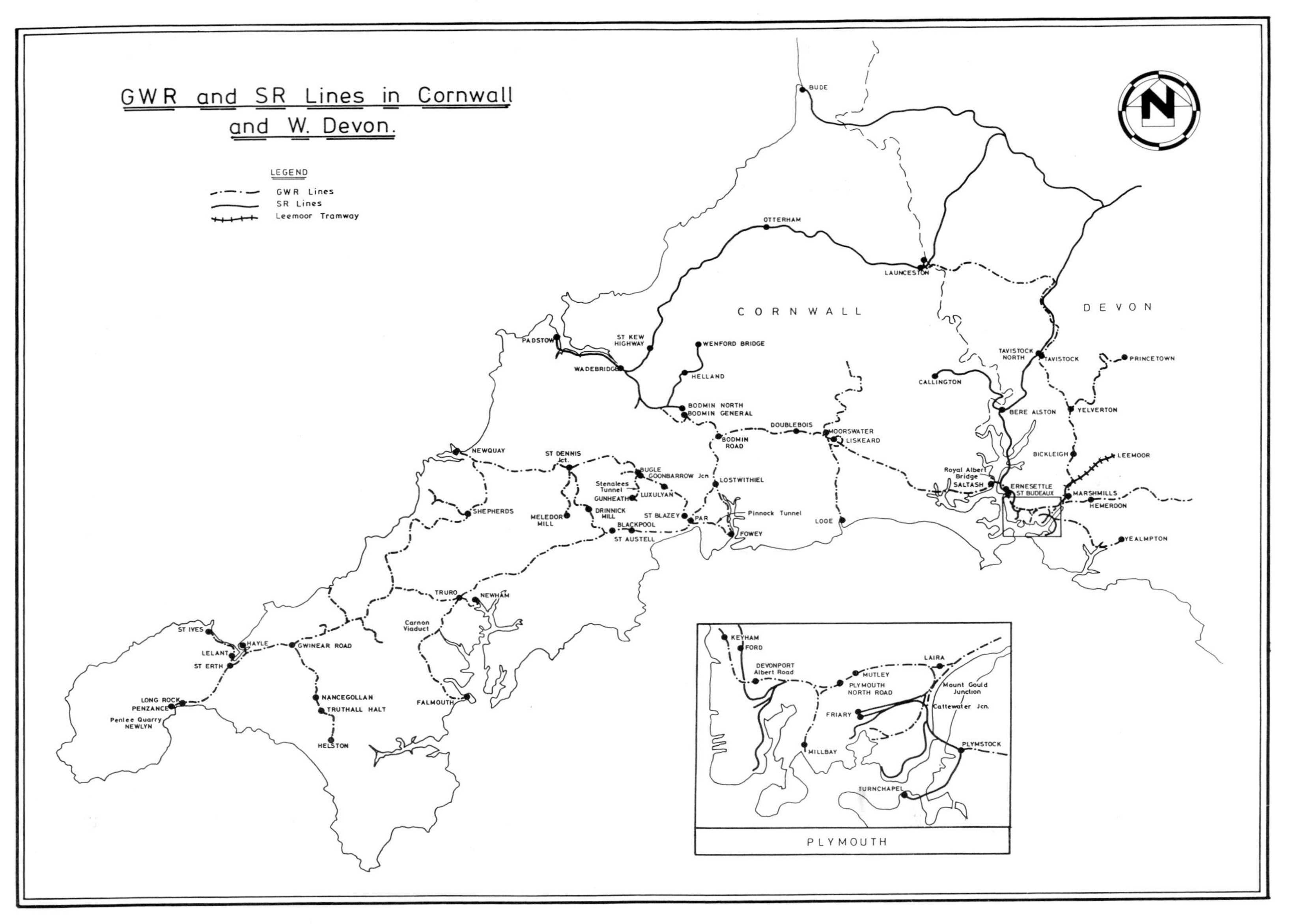
GWR and SR Lines in Cornwall and W. Devon.
LEGEND
GWR Lines
SR Lines
Leemoor Tramway
CORNWALL
DEVON
BUDE
OTTERHAM
LAUNCESTON
PADSTOW
ST KEW HIGHWAY
WADEBRIDGE
WENFORD BRIDGE
HELLAND
BODMIN NORTH
BODMIN GENERAL
BODMIN ROAD
DOUBLEBOIS
MOORSWATER
LISKEARD
LOSTWITHIEL
Pinnock Tunnel
FOWEY
LOOE
PAR
ST BLAZEY
BUGLE
GOONBARROW Jcn
Stenalees Tunnel
LUXULYAN
GUNHEATH
DRINNICK MILL
BLACKPOOL
ST AUSTELL
MELEDOR MILL
ST DENNIS Jct.
NEWQUAY
SHEPHERDS
TRURO
NEWHAM
Carnon Viaduct
FALMOUTH
ST IVES
LELANT
ST ERTH
HAYLE
GWINEAR ROAD
NANCEGOLLAN
TRUTHALL HALT
HELSTON
LONG ROCK
PENZANCE
Penlee Quarry
NEWLYN
CALLINGTON
TAVISTOCK NORTH
TAVISTOCK
PRINCETOWN
YELVERTON
BERE ALSTON
BICKLEIGH
LEEMOOR
Royal Albert Bridge
SALTASH
ERNESETTLE
ST BUDEAUX
MARSHMILLS
HEMERDON
YEALMPTON
KEYHAM
FORD
DEVONPORT Albert Road
MUTLEY
PLYMOUTH NORTH ROAD
LAIRA
Mount Gould Junction
Cattewater Jcn.
FRIARY
MILLBAY
PLYMSTOCK
TURNCHAPEL
PLYMOUTH

A challenge to steam as Metrovic Gas Turbine 18100 prepares to descend Hemerdon bank with the 1.30 p.m. Paddington–Penzance on 5.9.52.

The 12.25 p.m. Penzance–Kensington milk train clears the top of Hemerdon bank – 2 miles at 1:42/41 pulled by 'Hall' class 4–6–0 5962 *Wantage Hall* (Old Oak Common) piloted by 'Castle' class 4–6–0 4098 *Kidwelly Castle* (Laira) on 5.9.52.

With a marvellous assortment of stock in tow the 4.42 p.m. Plymouth North Road–Paddington parcels comes over the top of Hemerdon bank on 5.9.52 hauled by 'Castle' class 4–6–0 7019 *Fowey Castle* (Bath Road, Bristol) piloted by 'Manor' class 4–6–0 7804 *Baydon Manor* (Laira).

A final steam working out of Plymouth North Road took place when Ian Allan ran his 'Great Western Limited' on 9.5.64. 'Castle' class 4–6–0 7029 *Clun Castle* bursts through the bridge at the top of Hemerdon having performed the climb unassisted but using maximum effort.

Bickleigh station on the Tavistock (Launceston) branch with 'Grange' class 4–6–0 6870 *Bodicote Grange* (Penzance) on what would appear to be a Royal Marine Commando special on 21.8.59.

Roy Taylor

Yelverton with a 4400 class 2–6–2T entering the turntable road, the procedure being that after depositing passengers from the Princetown branch on the platform the loco would propel the stock on to the branch, and the guard would apply the coach brakes. The loco would uncouple, shunt back and run forward into the turntable road, clear of both sets of points, after which the brakes would be partially released to allow the stock to gravitate back into the station, the loco then backing out on to its train. Clerestory stock remained in use on the Princetown branch until 1946.

Lens of Sutton

The last passenger trains on the Princetown branch ran on 3.3.56 and from mid-afternoon were double-headed by 4575 class 2–6–2T 4583, assisted by 4500 class 2–6–2T 4568, both from Laira shed, seen here on the 2.56 p.m. Yelverton–Princetown in desolate country, typical of the line, with both locos working hard in wet and very windy conditions tackling the nearly continuous 1:40 gradient.

Lens of Sutton

Princetown was the highest station on the GWR system, its height variously quoted as 1373, 1395 and 1410 ft. 4500 class 2–6–2T 4542 of Laira shed waits to depart from the moorland terminus during the last summer of the line's life, the summer of 1955. 4500 class locos succeeded the 4400 class tanks during the last six months.

Lens of Sutton

The 6.20 p.m. Plymouth North Road–Launceston of 29.12.62 reached Tavistock South at 12.25 a.m. the next day after battling through a blizzard. This was the last passenger service to traverse the line and was unable to proceed further as the line beyond was blocked by a snowdrift in a deep cutting. Still carrying the funeral wreath on the smoke-box door, 4575 class 2–6–2T 5568 of Laira shed is frozen to the track at Tavistock on 30.12.62 at 9.30 a.m. The fire had to be dropped as the water in the tank seen here became frozen.

6400 class 0–6–0PT 6407 of Laira shed stands beneath the overall roof of Tavistock South with the 4.30 p.m. auto working to Plymouth North Road on 25.6.55.

4575 class 2–6–2T 5572 of Laira shed shunts at Launceston with the goods from Tavistock junction, the photograph being taken from a 'Down' SR train leaving Launceston on 1.1.60.

English China Clays operated a fireless loco at their Marsh Mills Driers, the last operational steam loco to work in revenue-earning service in the Plymouth area. Bagnall 3121 of 1957, an 0–4–0, replaced a Fowler diesel until being superseded itself in 1970. It is seen here at Marsh Mills on 9.8.67. This loco has been preserved; first at the Bugle Steam Railway and now at Bodmin General station.

4575 class 2–6–2T 5531 of Laira shed on the turntable at the SR engine shed at Launceston after working the 3.50 p.m. passenger from Plymouth North Road on 25.6.55. GWR engines turned at the SR shed although one was stabled in the GW shed overnight and at weekends.

4575 class 2–6–2T 5572 of Laira stands at Launceston SR with a train from Plymouth on 21.10.61, a wet day. A connection between the GWR and SR at Launceston was opened on 22.9.43 and using this, WR passenger trains terminated at the SR station from 30.6.52. The signal-box with a frame each side is visible on the 'Down' SR platform, and beyond is the GWR loco shed. Note the goods traffic in the SR yard. The engine has had a 'top up' from the water column and the fireman is securing the inlet cover.

Terry Nicholls

The interior of Laira junction signal-box in the summer of 1960 with the 116 lever frame, indicator panel and wheel which worked the gates guarding the Lee Moor Tramway level crossing. This box is now just a memory.

Denis Richards

The view west from Laira junction signal-box in May 1961 with 'The First Cornish New Potato Special' passing hauled by 'County' class 4–6–0 1001 *County of Bucks*, a Laira engine. Laira shed is on the left with plenty of locos in evidence.

Larry Crosier

Laira junction with 'Grange' class 4–6–0 6849 *Walton Grange* of Laira shed tackling the 1:67 climb to Mutley tunnel with the 8.18 p.m. Tavistock junction–Truro goods on 14.5.60.

The 12.25 Penzance–Kensington milk train passing Laira Halt in June 1953, hauled by 4700 class 2–8–0 4701 from Old Oak Common shed and piloted by 'Castle' class 4–6–0 4077 *Chepstow Castle* of Newton Abbot shed. Note the typical GWR 'pagoda' shelter on the 'Up' platform; the station closed to passengers on 7.7.30 and the 'Down' platform was removed.

6400 class 0–6–0PT 6419 of Laira shed passing Lipson junction on 14.5.60 with the 7.10 p.m. Rail-Motor from Tavistock South to Plymouth North Road. Lipson junction signal-box is in the background.

Looking down on 'King' class 4–6–0 6000 *King George V* from the coaler ramp on 27.5.62. For many years this engine was shedded at Laira but by now had moved to Old Oak Common. Note the bell above the front buffers and the commemorative medals above the cabside numberplate, together with the double blastpipe modification. The adjacent track was the 'ash road' used by a steam crane.

'Castle' class 4–6–0 5069 *Isambard Kingdom Brunel* stands outside the front of the 'long' or 'new' shed at Laira on 22.11.59. This was one of the locos maintained in exceptional mechanical condition and kept spotlessly clean by Laira for working the 'Ocean Liner Specials' from Millbay Docks to Paddington. This select band of 'Castles' were known as 'Boat Engines'. Two more 'Castles' are in the yard and a 'Warship' diesel is partially out of the shed; two of the four roads of which had been walled off for use by the newly arrived diesel locos.

'Star' class 4–6–0 4051 *Princess Helena* from Worcester shed – a rare visitor to Laira – on the coaling line on a summer Saturday in August 1950. The shedman is watching 'King' class loco 6021 *King Richard II* – a visitor from Old Oak Common – buffer up to the tender of the 'Star'. The Star was withdrawn the following October.

'Grange' class 4–6–0 6804 *Brockington Grange* from St Phillips Marsh shed (Bristol), in the yard at Laira in June 1953.

A line-up of engines awaiting coaling at Laira on the evening of 20.4.55. In order these are 'Grange' class 4–6–0 6820 *Kingstone Grange* from Newport Ebbw junction shed, a 'Modified Hall', another 'Grange' and an 8750 class pannier tank. The shedman is opening the smoke-box door of the 'Hall'.

One of Churchward's big 4700 class 2–8–0s – 4700 itself from Old Oak Common shed – backs away from the roundhouse on 19.6.60 after coaling at Laira. A 'Hall' is in the background.

A trio of 'Oil-Burners' at their home shed Laira in September 1947 in spotless external condition: 2800 class 2–8–0 4808 (ex 2834) stands ahead of 4807 (ex 2848) while behind is 'Hall' class 4–6–0 3904 *Saint Brides Hall* (ex 4972). Note the LA stencil on the frame below the steam pipe.

2884 class 2–8–0 3856 from Southall shed in June 1953 at Laira after coaling, while on the coaling line, having worked in on the 'Down Limited' (Cornish Riviera) is 'King' class 4–6–0 6009 *King Charles II* from Old Oak Common shed. An interesting PW train is on the embankment.

A stranger to Laira in June 1953 was this LMS design 2P/2F 2–6–0 46526 built at Swindon and newly allocated to St Phillips Marsh shed, Bristol which had worked in on 'The Swindon Fish' – a favourite turn for running in new or overhauled engines. At the rear is an engine from Old Oak Common shed, 'King' class 4–6–0 6009 *King Charles II.*

A big surprise at Laira on 16.4.54 was this Swindon-built Standard class 3 2–6–0 77006 which had used 'The Swindon Fish' as a running-in turn. This loco was subsequently allocated to Hamilton shed, but before that it visited Laira again, as did also 77005.

Inside the roundhouse at Laira on 22.11.59 are three tank locos: 8750 class 0–6–0PTs 3790 and 9716 with 4575 class 2–6–2T 4591 adorned with a GWR-type buffer beam number and the LA shed stencil. It is believed that this was carried out at Launceston shed during weekends. Other locos were also treated, including 4549 and 4592. 4591 spent most of its life at Laira working the Launceston branch.

5100 class 2–6–2T 5148 on 22.11.59 – a Laira engine and the last member of the class at its home shed – around the back of the coaler. Notice the somewhat buckled frame caused by banking freight trains up to Hemerdon. At the rear is St Blazey 7400 class 0–6–0PT 7446, probably *en route* to Newton Abbot Factory.

Newly transferred from Wellington shed (actually sub-shedded at Much Wenlock), still bearing the WLN shed stencil with a Laira 83D shedplate, is 4400 class 2–6–2T 4403 on 6.5.51 coming on to the coaling line at Laira shed. These engines, with their 4 ft $1\frac{1}{2}$ in driving wheels were staple power for the Princetown branch for many years, which abounded in sharp curves with an almost continuous rising gradient of 1:40 for $10\frac{1}{2}$ miles.

Mid-evening at Laira shed on 14.5.60 and a light is on. 1361 class 0–6–0ST 1363 awaits coaling after duties in Millbay Docks, for which Laira possessed four of the five members of the class for many years. One Christmas Day in the early fifties all five members were in Laira roundhouse. 8750 class 0–6–0PT 3787 is on coal bank duty.

Laira shed's coaling and reception lines on a summer Saturday afternoon in September 1949. By mid-evening engines would be lined up stretching out past Laira junction signal-box in the background. Visible from left to right with the engines' home shed in brackets are 'County' class 4–6–0 1026 *County of Salop* (Old Oak Common), 8750 class 0–6–0PT 9716 (Laira), 'Hall' class 4–6–0 5990 *Dorford Hall* (Gloucester), 1901 class 0–6–0PT 1990 (Laira) and 3150 class 2–6–2T 3178 (Laira) – 1990 was withdrawn two months later.

4575 class 2–6–2T 5567 of Laira shed leaves the west end of Mutley tunnel with the 5.40 p.m. Launceston–Plymouth North Road (on to Millbay as ECS) on 15.6.56. This end of the tunnel is now obscured by an over-line car park.

'Britannia' class 4–6–2 Pacific 70021 *Morning Star* of Laira shed in the Park sidings at Plymouth North Road in April 1952 waiting to attach the Plymouth portion to the 1.10 p.m. Penzance–Paddington, which it would work forward departing at 4.10 p.m. and arriving at Paddington at 9.00 p.m.

'King' class 4–6–0 6023 *King Edward II* from Laira shed waits to leave Plymouth North Road for Laira in August 1950 after working the 7.30 a.m. Paddington–Plymouth. The size of the boiler can be appreciated in this photograph.

'King' class 4–6–0 6012 *King Edward VI* of Old Oak Common shed on 9.3.59 waiting to depart from Plymouth North Road for Paddington with the 'Up' 'Royal Duchy' – 11.00 a.m. ex Penzance.
The late Edward George Dart

The Brown–Boveri gas turbine loco 18000 entering Plymouth North Road on its first trial run to Devon on 22.2.50.

'Hall' class 4–6–0 6949 *Haberfield Hall* of Laira shed at Plymouth North Road with the 1.12 p.m. to Liverpool Lime Street on 9.3.59.

The late Edward George Dart

The 9.00 a.m. Wolverhampton (Low Level) to Penzance entering Plymouth North Road on 25.5.57 hauled by 'Castle' class 4–6–0 5079 *Lysander* of Newton Abbot shed, piloted by 'Manor' class 4–6–0 7820 *Dinmore Manor* of Laira shed.

'Saint' class 4–6–0 2934 *Butleigh Court* from Swindon shed pilots a 'Modified Hall' out of Plymouth North Road on the 4.42 p.m. perishables to Paddington in April 1952. This loco was withdrawn two months later.

'Grange' class 4–6–0 6849 *Walton Grange* of Laira shed leaves Plymouth North Road on 4.4.59 with the 1.55 p.m. Penzance–Newton Abbot stopping service which called at all stations.

North British 'Warship' class diesel hydraulic D601 *Ark Royal* being towed through Plymouth North Road by 4300 class 2–6–0 6319 after failing on the 'Up Limited' on 14.6.58. Both locos were shedded at Laira, where they are bound.

A pair of 2–6–2Ts double-head the 2.55 p.m. ex Plymouth Millbay on 14.7.62 into North Road to form the 3.05 p.m. to Launceston, the leading engine being detached at North Road, having assisted up the 1:51 incline. The engines, both from Laira shed, are 4500 class 4570 and 4575 class 5568.

6400 class 0–6–0PT 6406 of Laira shed waits at North Road in August 1951 to run to Laira auto-car sidings with 2.47 p.m. ECS working.

3150 class 2–6–2T 3186 of Laira shed proceeds around Lipson No. 1 curve with the 1.35 p.m. ENPARTS train from Laira shed to Plymouth Millbay in the mid-fifties. Laira yard is in the background on the site now occupied by Laira diesel depot.

Mike Daly

M7 class 0–4–4T 30036 of Friary shed waits to depart from Plymouth North Road with the 5.27 p.m. local train to Tavistock North on 5.8.61.

1361 class 0–6–0ST 1361 proceeds past North Road west to its home shed at Laira after completing Millbay Docks shunting duties in March 1952.

Laira yard on 6.7.58 showing 4 ft 6 in gauge Lee Moor Tramway trucks and crane wagons beside a vast assortment of standard gauge wagons and vans – a scene now vastly changed.

Plymouth Friary station in the mid-fifties with M7 0–4–4T 30036 of Friary shed shunting and a GW 4300 class 'Mogul' 2–6–0 awaiting its turn of duty. Two trains a day in each direction on GW and SR routes between Plymouth and Exeter were worked by engines and crews of the 'other' region to give route familiarization in case of blockages. This station closed to passengers 15.9.58 and is now a goods depot.

Lens of Sutton

Plymouth Friary yard with a T9 class 4–4–0 marshalling coaching stock in the late forties. The line between the low walls in the foreground dropped down an incline through a tunnel to serve North Quay and the Barbican area, and was worked by B4 class 0–4–0Ts.

Lens of Sutton

0395 class 0–6–0 30564 of Exmouth junction shed in Friary shed yard in the early fifties. These were infrequent visitors to Plymouth.

Mike Daly

Plymouth, Devonport and South Western junction railway 0–6–2T 30757 'Earl of Mount Edgcumbe' out of use in the early fifties at Friary shed where it was based for many years for Callington branch duties.

Mike Daly

PDSWJ 0–6–2T 30758 'Lord St Levan' on shed pilot duties at home at Friary in the early fifties.

Mike Daly

A pair of M7 0–4–4Ts on Friary shed, together with a B4 0–4–0T on 19.10.57. 30036, 30035 and 30088 are all based at Friary.

O2 class 0–4–4T 30183 in light steam at its home, Friary shed, on 16.4.54.

A train of timber from Bayleys wharf at Oreston comes off Laira bridge over the River Plym heading for Cattewater junction and Friary yard in August 1957. It is hauled by one of Friary shed's stud of B40–4–0Ts 30102.

Denis Richards

Plymouth Railway Circle ran a farewell train to Turnchapel, hauled by Friary-based M7 0–4–4T 30034 seen here on 30.9.61. After allowing those passengers so wishing to alight, the train reversed on to the swing bridge for photography. The bridge has been dismantled, but the piers remain protruding from the water of Hooe Lake.

Early morning activity in June 1957 at Friary shed where locally-based B4 0–4–0Ts 30083 and 30102 are prepared for their day's work on the Cattewater branch and Bayleys wharf siding at Oreston.
Denis Richards

Plymouth Railway Circle ran a final train to Yealmpton, seen here at the GWR platform at Plymstock on 27.2.60. It was hauled by 4500 class 2–6–2T 4549 of Laira shed which still retained inside steam pipes.

Plymouth Railway Circle's farewell brake van special on 27.2.60 at Yealmpton after the loco; Laira's 4500 class 2–6–2T 4549 had run around its train. The line in the background disappearing through the bridge was the start of the proposed extension to Modbury which was never constructed.

Laira sheds 1361 class 0–6–0ST 1363 shunting in the GWR Millbay docks in the late fifties. Note the fruit van and the GWR match truck.

Larry Crosier

Ford viaduct on the SR route between Ford (Devon) and Albert Road Halt on 4.3.61. This structure took six months to demolish as the pillars were found to consist of solid concrete encased in bricks and stone. On 7.9.64 this route closed completely.

A very rare shot showing the 'Up Limited' ('Cornish Riviera') approaching St Budeaux after diversion onto the SR route on 13.12.53. This was due to a breakaway and derailment of wagons on Dainton bank blocking the GW route. The train would have reversed at North Road and is in charge of Exeter-based 'Mogul' 7316 – heavier engines such as 'Halls' not being permitted to cross Meldon viaduct. This engine would have had to work very hard as the SR route to Exeter was moderately heavily graded with sharp curves. The wartime connection between the two routes is visible.

Bullied Light Pacific 34109 'Sir Trafford Leigh Mallory' of Exmouth junction shed pauses with a brake van in the SR yard at St Budeaux on 1.6.58.

O2 class 0–4–4T 30225 of Friary shed crosses the connection at St Budeaux from the SR to the GWR in the mid-fifties. The train started at Devonport Kings Road yard, reversed at St Budeaux Victoria Road and ran over GW metals to enter HM Dockyard – arriving at 10.05 a.m. on weekdays. Note the SR coaches berthed in St Budeaux yard, often used for this purpose.

Mike Daly

4300 class 'Mogul' 5376 of Laira shed has just passed below the GW line west of St Budeaux working the 2.35 p.m. Plymouth Friary–Exeter Central 'interchange' turn in January 1953.

St Budeaux Victoria Road with Light Pacific 34063 *229 Squadron* departing following blizzard conditions at 1.35 p.m. on 30.12.62. This train had set out from Friary in the morning to try and rescue three locos caught in a snowdrift at Sourton, near Bridestowe. It reached Tavistock North and returned to Plymouth with the crew and passengers off the stranded 6.20 p.m. Plymouth–Launceston of the previous night. No other trains ran on either route that day. The loco was from Exmouth junction shed.

A pair of Friary shed's M7 0–4–4Ts double-head a stopping train to Tavistock North in the early fifties. Passing west of St Budeaux on the SR route are 30039 and 30668. This was a means of working an engine to Tavistock for goods duties.

Mike Daly

The SR's version of a 'Double-Fairlie'! A pair of Friary shed's O2 class 0–4–4Ts double-head a Tavistock local in the early fifties. Passing west of St Budeaux Victoria Road are 30183 and s224 – as yet not renumbered. The front loco will shunt at Tavistock or change over duties on the Callington branch.

Mike Daly

Light Pacific 34038 'Lynton' passes Ernesettle beside the River Tamar with the 9.00 a.m. Waterloo–Friary express on 26.5.56. The engine is shedded at Friary and the photograph was taken from the Royal Albert Bridge during a Plymouth Railway Circle visit. On the extreme left is a freight train in Ernesettle siding.

N class 2–6–0 31830 from Exmouth junction shed enters Bere Alston with a Plymouth North Road to Exeter Central stopping service in September 1961. Behind the signal-box and fence are a pair of LM 2MT 2–6–2Ts, one on the Callington branch passenger service, the other either changing over or working the branch goods. On 6.5.68 services beyond here on the SR main line ceased.

Harry Cowan

O2 class 0–4–4T 30183, allocated to Friary shed but sub-shedded at Callington, is seen here outside the tiny shed in June 1961. Callington station is in the background.

Harry Cowan

One of Friary shed's O2 class 0–4–4Ts 30225 at Bere Alston awaiting departure with a Callington branch train in the mid-fifties. On 7.11.66 the Callington branch closed beyond Gunnislake.

Lens of Sutton

Friary-allocated 2MT 2–6–2T 41316 at Callington preparing to leave for Bere Alston with the branch goods in the late fifties.

Lens of Sutton

'Grange' class 4–6–0 6868 *Penrhos Grange*, shedded at Penzance, passes through Devonport Albert Road with the 11.30 a.m. Tavistock junction–Penzance freight on 24.11.61.

Larry Crosier

Light Pacific 34063 *229 Squadron* waits to return to Friary from Tavistock North on 30.12.62 at 1.01 p.m. The train, bound for Sourton to rescue locos in a snowdrift, was unable to enter the station at Tavistock until the railwaymen aboard, assisted by a dozen railway enthusiasts, stranded on the previous day's 6.20 p.m. Plymouth–Launceston WR train, cleared the tracks and pointwork of snow. The train stopped on the viaduct at 10.45 a.m., departed at 1.02 p.m. and ran wrong line to Bere Alston terminating, it is thought, at Devonport Kings Road.

'The Last Days of Steam' in another sense. Although a bit earlier than the scope of the book this is a very rare photograph depicting 'Hall' class 4–6–0 4911 *Bowden Hall*, a Penzance-allocated engine, at Keyham station, after a German blitz raid during the night of 28/9.4.41. This loco was officially withdrawn in June 1941.

Maurice Dart collection

The engine shed at HM Dockyard Devonport in the summer of 1950. The Avonside Engine loco outside is No. 12 and the pair of Andrew Barclay locos in the shed are No. 13 and either 17 or 18. On 10.10.82 most of this system, including the tunnel, closed.

Mike Daly

Weston Mill viaduct over Camel's Head creek on 20.9.58, known locally as 'Shaky Bridge', between Keyham and St Budeaux, is also a footbridge; the walkway being on the opposite side to that shown.

A Laira engine, 6400 class 0–6–0PT 6407, approaches St Budeaux East with an afternoon Plymouth–Saltash 'Auto-working' in April 1955. These were announced at North Road as 'Rail-cars' and the public called them 'Motor-trains'.

'Grange' class 4–6–0 6801 *Aylburton Grange* approaches St Budeaux East in April 1955 running light engine to Penzance where it was shedded for many years, being the first of the class to be withdrawn in October 1960.

'Grange' class 4–6–0 6801 *Aylburton Grange* approaching St Budeaux East at speed on the 'Down Limited' in April 1950. The 'Cornish Riviera' was often entrusted to one of this superb class of engine which, with their 5 ft 8 in driving wheels, performed admirably on the Cornish banks. Sadly not one of the eighty members of the class was preserved.

'Mogul' 6319 of Laira shed approaching St Budeaux East on the 10.40 p.m. Paddington–Penzance parcels working on 20.9.58.

6400 class 0–6–0PT 6420, a Laira engine, passing St Budeaux East with a Saltash–North Road Auto-train on 1.12.57.

An extremely rare photograph of a Naval Personnel Leave special on 13.12.53 which had started from Admiralty platform on the branch line to HM Dockyard, to run to Birmingham. Dainton bank was blocked by debris from a freight train breakaway so WR trains were diverted up the SR route, most reversing at North Road. However, this fourteen-coach train used the wartime connection at St Budeaux East which it is seen here traversing, hauled by a pair of GW 'Moguls' 5339 of Newton Abbot shed and piloted by 6319 from Laira. The run to Exeter would have been most exciting for a railway enthusiast but extremely hard work for the two locos and their crews.

'Grange' class 4–6–0 6808 *Beenham Grange* of Penzance shed passing St Budeaux East on the 'Up Limited' on 13.12.53. This particular engine was regarded by local drivers as being 'one coach stronger' than other members of the class and was shedded at Penzance for about twenty-three years. The Bullpoint branch is bottom left.

When the Cardiff Valley's interval services were converted to diesel, the auto-fitted Prairie tanks were dispersed, so 4575 class 2–6–2T 5560 was transferred from Tondu to Laira and is seen here on 17.5.61 leaving St Budeaux Ferry Road with the 6.37 p.m. North Road–St Germans Rail-Motor train.

6400 class 0–6–0PT 6413 transferred from Aberdare via Oxford to Laira propels the Sunday 11.25 a.m. North Road–Saltash Rail-Motor past St Budeaux West, having just crossed above the SR main line on 4.6.60.

An engine shedded at Penzance for many years was 'Hall' class 4–6–0 5915 *Trentham Hall* seen here climbing the 1:79 past St Budeaux West (signal-box visible above train) with the 1.45 p.m. Tavistock junction–Penzance freight in January 1953. The engine has been fitted with one of the new pattern straight-sided tenders.

3150 class 2–6–2T 3187 of Laira shed passing St Budeaux West with an assortment of wagons and vans on the 9.25 a.m. Tavistock junction–St Austell goods in the early fifties.
Mike Daly

'Grange' class 4–6–0 6824 *Ashley Grange* of Penzance shed approaching St Budeaux West with the 12.45 p.m. St Blazey–Tavistock junction freight working in January 1953.

The fireman on 'Grange' class 4–6–0 6838 *Goodmoor Grange* of Penzance shed picks up the token as they pass Royal Albert Bridge signal-box with the 1.30 p.m. Paddington–Penzance on 7.8.55. It is only single track across the bridge.

'Grange' class 4–6–0 6875 *Hindford Grange* of Penzance shed comes off the Royal Albert Bridge with the 12.45 p.m. St Blazey–Tavistock junction freight train on 10.7.60 as the signalman leans out of the box to collect the token from the fireman. Construction of the Tamar Road Bridge has commenced.

The late Edward George Dart

Signalman Martin Dennis pulls off the Down Distant in Royal Albert Bridge signal-box late on the wet evening of 3.5.59. The box still stands and is used by bridge engineers.

Looking down on 6400 class 0–6–0PT 6421 of Laira shed working the 3.05 p.m. Saltash–North Road Auto-train on 26.5.56, taken from the Devon entrance to the bridge tubes during a Plymouth Railway Circle visit.

A 'Grange' class 4–6–0 crosses Forder viaduct with a 'Down' train between Saltash and St Germans on 31.7.59.

Peter Gray

Laira 6400 class 0–6–0PT 6421 enters Liskeard in a torrential downpour with the 5.50 p.m. Auto-train from North Road on 23.5.60.

A 6400 class 0–6–0PT sandwiched between Auto-cars at Saltash around 1960 waits to work to North Road. Note Wyman's bookstall.

C.H. Bastin

Laira 5700 class 0–6–0PT 8709 shunts at Liskeard in 1946/47, with the now demolished goods shed in the background. Notice the GWR number on the back buffer beam.

Revd Peter Witney

A St Blazey loco 4575 class 2–6–2T 5557 backs its train out of the Looe branch station at Liskeard in order to run around on 17.8.58.

Anthony Bennett

4575 class 2–6–2T 5551 of St Blazey takes water at Looe prior to working the 3.48 p.m. train to Liskeard on 1.8.59. This engine retained a tall safety-valve bonnet at this time.

A surviving relic of bygone days was this Cornwall Railway signal-box at Westwood siding in the Glyn Valley between Doublebois and Largin at the west end of Westwood viaduct on 15.6.61. It controlled a broad gauge siding into Westwood Quarry and in late June 1962 was demolished.

'Grange' class 4–6–0 6875 *Hindford Grange* of Penzance shed climbs across Clinnick viaduct in the Glyn Valley heading the 6.00 a.m. Penzance–Manchester on 8.8.59.

Peter Gray

Doublebois station with 'Castle' class 4–6–0 5021 *Whittington Castle*, a Laira engine, in charge of the 'Up' 'Royal Duchy', 11.00 a.m. Penzance–Paddington, on 4.7.59. On 7.12.64 this station closed to goods traffic, passengers having already ceased, and the site was cleared.

Peter Gray

On 26.6.56 'Hall' class 4–6–0 5915 *Trentham Hall* of Penzance shed runs into Bodmin Road on the 'Jubilee', the unofficial railwayman's name for the 3.30 p.m. Paddington–Penzance, while O2 class 0–4–4T 30236 of Wadebridge shed takes water after working the 8.40 p.m. train from Padstow forming the 9.50 p.m. to Wadebridge.

Wadebridge-allocated 8750 class 0–6–0PT 4666, still carrying an 87C Danygraig shed-plate, takes water at Bodmin Road after working the 6.01 p.m. from Bodmin General and returning with the 6.17 p.m. to Wadebridge on 21.8.61. The train leaving the platform is the 4.20 p.m. Penzance–Newton Abbot headed by twinned class 22 Diesel Hydraulics D6322 with D6312 as pilot – both allocated to Laira.

O2 class 0–4–4T 30200 allocated to Wadebridge shed, runs around its train, the 6.17 p.m. Bodmin Road–Wadebridge, at Bodmin General on 22.6.56. The goods shed, which has since been removed, is on the left. This route was closed on 21.11.83 but happily on 17.6.90 passenger services were restored between Bodmin Parkway and Bodmin General by a preservation society.

4500 class 2–6–2T 4526 allocated to St Blazey and sub-shedded at Bodmin outside the shed in the evening of 22.6.56.

Wadebridge-allocated O2 class 0–4–4T 30236 running round its train at Bodmin North prior to working the 6.43 p.m. to Padstow on 26.6.56. This section to Dunmere junction was closed on 30.1.67.

'Beattie Well' 2–4–0WT 30587 of Wadebridge shed at Helland wharf with a Plymouth Railway Circle brake van special from Wadebridge to Wenford Bridge on 31.5.58.

1366 class 0–6–0PT 1369 at Helland crossing with a Plymouth Railway Circle brake van special to Wenford Bridge on 19.9.64.

'Beattie Well' 2–4–0WT 30587 of Wadebridge shed shunting on the curve just below Wenford Bridge goods depot to the right of the photographer on 19.8.58. On 21.11.83 the Wenford branch closed completely.

Anthony Bennett

'Battle of Britain' class 4–6–2 34081 *92 Squadron* from Exmouth junction shed running into Wadebridge on 19.8.58 with the 'Down' 'Atlantic Coast Express'; the 10.50 a.m. Waterloo to various West-Country termini.

Anthony Bennett

Two Exmouth-junction T9 class 4–4–0s at Wadebridge on 5.6.57. 30711 is running in with the 5.51 p.m. Okehampton–Padstow while 30710 is on the left.

4575 class 2–6–2T 5502 of St Blazey shed at Wadebridge with the 8.42 p.m. service to Bodmin Road on 24.7.56.

'Beattie Well' 2–4–0T 30586 shunts at Wadebridge, its home station, in the late fifties.
George Hemmett

Wadebridge's 8750 class 0–6–0PT 4666 waits to leave its home station with the 12.42 p.m. to Bodmin North on 1.1.60.

Wadebridge-based 1366 class 0–6–0PT 1368 shunts the yard in the early sixties. These outside cylinder pannier tanks replaced the 'Beattie Well' tanks.

George Hemmett

U class 2–6–0 31804 shedded at Exmouth junction stands outside the back of Wadebridge shed on 24.7.56.

N class 2–6–0 31841 shedded at Exmouth junction stands outside the back of Wadebridge shed on 5.6.57.

T9 class 4–4–0 30718 from Exmouth junction stands outside the back of Wadebridge shed on 1.1.60.

Wadebridge shed on 31.5.58, the day it was visited by Plymouth Railway Circle. The three local engines lined up are 'Beattie Well' 2–4–0WTs 30585 and 30586 with O2 class 0–4–4T 30236 while Exmouth junction's N class 2–6–0 31840 stands outside the shed.

'Beattie Well' 2–4–0WT 30587 under the hoist at Wadebridge shed after a side collision in August 1957.

Terry Nicholls

Exmouth junction-based T9 class 4–4–0 30708, actually sub-shedded at Okehampton, runs around the 5.51 p.m. from Okehampton at Padstow on 26.6.56. The complete closure of the route to Padstow took place on 30.1.67.

Exmouth junction's T9 class 4-4-0 30715 in the carriage sidings at Padstow in September 1961.
Harry Cowan

T9 class 4-4-0 120 worked a Plymouth Railway Circle/RCTS special from Exeter Central to Padstow and seen here at Otterham on 27.4.63.

N class 2–6–0 31844 of Exmouth junction shed runs into Launceston on an 'Up' passenger working on 21.10.61. This route closed on 3.10.66.

Terry Nicholls

'Mickey Mouse' 2MT 2–6–2T 82030 of Exmouth junction shed backing on to its train at Bude, the most northerly station in Cornwall, at the end of the branch line from Halwill on 21.11.64.
Terry Nicholls

Exmouth junction shed's 'Mickey Mouse' 2MT 2–6–2T 82030 samples the shelter of Bude engine shed on 21.11.64. Bude engine shed was closed on 3.10.66.

Terry Nicholls

The identity of this 4575 class 2–6–2T in the milk siding at Lostwithiel is 5564 of St Blazey shed just ex Newton Abbot factory. It is waiting to attach milk tanks to the rear of the 12.20 p.m. Penzance–Kensington on 4.6.60.

'Castle' class 4–6–0 5011 *Tintagel Castle* from Newton Abbot shed brings a 'Down' express over Lostwithiel level crossing in the mid-fifties. Note the vans in the milk factory yard and the Western National bus waiting to depart, also the extension arm on the water column at the back of the 'Up' platform.

Maurice Dart collection

4575 class 2–6–2T 5573 from Newton Abbot comes through Lostwithiel 'light engine' heading for St Blazey for a short period on loan on 21.8.61.

The driver uses the oil can while the fireman hangs over the cab door on St Blazey's 4800 class 0–4–2T 1419, re-numbered from 4819 in October 1946. This is the Fowey branch train in the bay platform at Lostwithiel in the mid-fifties. On 4.1.65 this service was withdrawn.

Maurice Dart collection

'County' class 4–6–0 1015 *County of Gloucester* shedded at Laira brings the 2.50 p.m. Penzance–Paddington freight down the bank into Lostwithiel in the mid-fifties. Note the old wooden goods shed with loading gauge outside.

Maurice Dart collection

St Blazey shed's 4800 class 0–4–2T 1419 stands outside Fowey station while a class 22 D63XX Diesel Hydraulic waits in the sidings before proceeding via Pinnock tunnel to St Blazey yard in the early sixties.

George Hemmett

4200 class 2–8–0T 4273 shedded at St Blazey halts with a loaded clay train by Fowey station after descending the 1:36 incline from Pinnock tunnel in the mid-fifties. St Blazey shed usually possessed two of this class for working the steeply-graded route between Fowey and St Blazey.
George Hemmett

The Par portal of Pinnock tunnel, which is 1173 yds long and the longest railway tunnel west of Bristol on the GWR and Honiton on the SR, on 5.5.57. It was closed on 1.7.68 and converted to a road for use by clay lorries.

4200 class 2–8–0T 4247 from St Blazey eases a train of empty vans, used for moving clay in bags, along the line from Polmear Bridge to Five Arches past the back of Par beach on 10.7.57.

English China Clays operated locos at Par Harbour and, as one line on the system passed beneath a low bridge under the GWR main line, these had to be of low clearance. Here is *Bagnall* 0–4–0ST 2572, built in 1937 and later named *Judy*, shunting on the harbour on 7.8.56. Cornwall Mills, in the background, was destroyed in a fire several years later.

Another of St Blazey shed's allocation of 4200 class 2–8–0Ts 4294 brings empty clay wagons across Par beach *en route* from Fowey Jetties to St Blazey yard on 24.7.58.

Terry Nicholls

An earlier loco owned by English China Clays at Par Harbour was 'Sentinel' 4wVBT 6520 of 1927, previously named *Toby*, seen here on 10.7.57 out of use behind the loco shed. By about September 1977 the internal rail system had ceased to be used.

Par station with a Saturdays only train from Newquay, in charge of class 22 Diesel Hydraulic D6308 piloted by 'Grange' class 4–6–0 6812 *Chesford Grange*, both allocated to Laira shed, on 17.6.61. There would appear to be some consultation in progress – was the diesel in trouble?

One of St Blazey shed's engines 'washing its feet'. 5101 class 2–6–2T 5174 in floods at Par station following heavy rain on 22.1.59.

George Hemmett

A Truro engine, 4575 class 2–6–2T 5509 on the front of a Newquay train sheltering inside the goods shed at Par, now demolished, on 21.8.61.

The 9.30 a.m. to Newquay at Par station in very wet weather on 12.11.60 in charge of St Blazey 8750 class 0–6–0PT 9680. Two young boys, impervious to the downpour, watch the crew clad in storm coats.

'Grange' class 4–6–0 6826 *Nannerth Grange* – a Penzance engine brings the 6.20 p.m. Penzance–Kensington milk train down the bank into Par on 16.7.62.

Problems at Par station on 30.9.59 with the 10.30 p.m. Liverpool Lime Street–Penzance, which had been hauled by two of Laira's class 22 Diesel Hydraulics from Plymouth North Road. D6304 failed and D6301 struggled on, but at Par both were removed by 'Hall' class 4–6–0 6931 *Aldborough Hall* of Truro shed which took the train forward.

Running Foreman Fred Bishop with his clerk wearing cycle clips stands in front of St Blazey shed's 'Manor' class 4–6–0 7816 *Frilsham Manor*, beside the turntable, on 5.9.59.

St Blazey shed, an ex Cornwall Minerals Railway establishment, was a nine road part roundhouse, access to which was via the turntable outside. Here we see a section of the shed on 26.10.58 with 5700 class 0–6–0PT 8733, 5101 class 2–6–2T 5193 (Truro shed) and an 8750 class pannier inside.

4500 class 2–6–2T 4552 at its home shed of St Blazey beside the wagon works awaiting attention on 13.6.56. The wheels in front of the engine are from clay wagons. The hoist can be seen in the background.

One of St Blazey shed's 4575 class 2–6–2Ts 5519 on the vacuum-operated turntable before going inside the shed on 3.7.57.

The hoist at St Blazey shed with a collection of pannier tanks receiving attention to their wheels on 5.6.61. The tight curves on the clay lines caused excessive wear on the flanges. Local 0–6–0PTs with wheels removed are 5700 class 8702 and 7400 class 7446, with 8750 class 4665 visible alongside.

A visitor to St Blazey's 'factory', the GWR term for loco works, large or small, was 4800 class 0–4–2T 1427 of Newton Abbot shed on 7.8.56. Three of the roundhouse roads extended beyond, into this 'cathedral-like' workshop, where the evening sun permeated the deep shadows.

Three 2–6–2Ts stored out of use at St Blazey shed behind the coaler on 16.7.62, and superseded by diesels. They are 4500 class 4564 with 4575 class 5531 and 5518.

A pair of 'Grange' 4–6–0s descend Luxulyan bank with the 10.00 a.m. Newquay–Paddington on 19.7.58. They are 6873 *Caradoc Grange* (pilot) of Laira shed and 6805 *Broughton Grange* of Truro shed.

Peter Gray

Two other steam locos were at St Blazey on 16.7.62. Both had been withdrawn and dumped beside the wagon works. They were 5700 class 0–6–0PT 8719 and 4575 class 2–6–2T 5539.

The 9.30 a.m. Paddington–Newquay on 27.8.60 climbs out of the tunnel at the top of the three miles at 1:35/40 of Luxulyan bank headed by a pair of 4–6–0s. 'Grange' class 6854 *Roundhill Grange* of Penzance shed is the pilot assisting 'County' class 1006 *County of Cornwall* from Laira shed.

George Hemmett

1600 class 0–6–0PT 1626 passing the south end of Luxulyan station with the 2.30 p.m. Goonbarrow-branch clay train on 14.9.60. The signal-box and a clerestory-roofed camping coach are behind.

George Hemmett

1600 class 0–6–0PT 1626 slowly drifts into Luxulyan with the 2.30 p.m. Goonbarrow-branch clay train bound for St Blazey yard on 14.9.60. The siding on the right ran to a loading wharf, which was served by the narrow gauge Treskilling Kiln tramway.

George Hemmett

350 HP Diesel shunter D4008 allocated to St Blazey eases a clay train from the Goonbarrow branch on to the Newquay branch at Goonbarrow junction on 4.7.61. This scene has vastly changed since the construction of the Rocks Driers complex.

The western portal of Stenalees tunnel, 341 yds long, on the Goonbarrow branch on 24.11.56 showing the line climbing out on a gradient of 1:40. This line was closed beyond New Caudledown on 29.4.65 and beyond Wheal Henry on 3.12.78; only a stub remains.

A Plymouth Railway Circle brake van special ran from Fowey through Pinnock tunnel via St Blazey to cover the Goonbarrow branch. At Gunheath it was necessary to split the train before the 1:35 descent to Carbean siding. Here 1626 pauses on the 1:40 drop to the reversal at Gunheath on 22.4.61. Note the Carbean branch just showing (middle right) and New Caudledown tip (centre left).

One of St Blazey shed's small tank 45s 4500 class 2–6–2T 4559 starts away from Bugle with the 3.50 p.m. Par–Newquay on 24.11.56.

4500 class 2–6–2T 4526 with the Plymouth Railway Circle brake van special taking water at Drinnick Mill on 1.10.55. The branch to Nanpean wharf diverges left where the railwaymen are standing and Drinnick Mill North ground frame can be seen on the right.

4500 class 2–6–2T 4526 on 1.10.55 with Plymouth Railway Circle's brake van special at Melador Mill, the terminus of the Retew branch, beyond which a siding passed over a level crossing to serve The New Cornish Melador China Clay Company siding, this still being *in situ*. Exact closure details are uncertain but on 3.4.82 it was deleted from the WR sectional appendix.

Newquay station with 5101 class 2–6–2T 4167 of St Blazey shed and 4575 class 2–6–2T 4587 of Truro shed on trains to Par and Truro via Perranporth and Chacewater on 17.8.58.

Anthony Bennett

At Newquay on 26.7.58 waiting to depart is Laira's 'Modified Hall' class 4–6–0 7909 *Heveningham Hall* on a through working to Plymouth North Road.

Terry Nicholls

A Penzance engine for many years was 'Grange' class 4–6–0 6825 *Llanvair Grange* seen climbing the final 1:57 of the four mile bank from Par to St Austell with the 1.15 p.m. Bristol–Penzance on 8.4.58.

The 'new order' seen on 30.4.58, with the North British *Warship* Diesel Hydraulic D600 'Active', allocated to Laira, at St Austell with the 'Up Postal' service 6.40 p.m. Penzance–Paddington.

'County' class 4–6–0 1006 *County of Cornwall*, a Laira engine, starts away from St Austell with an 'Up' passenger working on 21.5.60.

Mike Daly

An engine shedded at Penzance for most of its life was 'Modified Hall' class 4–6–0 7925 *Westol Hall* seen here starting away from St Austell with the 1.30 p.m. Paddington–Penzance on 26.7.56.

One of Laira shed's stud of 'Castle' class 4–6–0s kept in immaculate condition. One of the 'Boat Engines' is seen here leaving St Austell with the 1.27 p.m. Paddington–Penzance Relief on 4.6.60. The engine is 5058 *Earl of Clancarty*.

A pair of class 22 Diesel Hydraulics in trouble on the 6.50 a.m. Plymouth–Penzance on 25.4.60. D6322 was pilot to D6312 which had failed, so these Laira diesels were assisted from Par by a St Blazey engine in the shape of 5101 class 2–6–2T 4167 seen here pulling away from St Austell.

4300 class 'Mogul' 2–6–0 6397 from St Blazey shed approaching St Austell with the 7.50 p.m. Penzance–Tavistock junction freight on 2.8.56.

Not a steam loco – even though there is a false chimney on this derelict engine – a Rushton and Proctor paraffin burner, a rare type, at Blackpool China Clay pit, near St Austell on 24.11.56. This was a 1000 mm gauge loco bought second-hand from the Cotton Powder Company Ltd, Kent in 1921. It was intended to be used to move 'overburden' from the pit to a tip but this was never initiated. The loco has been preserved.

Truro station with two Truro-based Prairie tanks. 4500 class 4508, still retaining inside steam pipes waits with the 7.35 p.m. to Falmouth, while 4575 class 4588 departs with the 7.15 p.m. to Newquay via Perranporth on 21.5.57.

4300 class 2–6–0 6300 of St Blazey shed climbs the 1:60 bank to Higher Town tunnel from Truro with a westbound freight on 21.5.57.

4575 class 2–6–2T 5526, based at Truro, awaits departure with the 7.00 p.m. to Falmouth in the bay platform at Truro on 21.5.57.

'County' class 4–6–0 1006 *County of Cornwall*, a Laira engine, pulls away from Truro up the bank with a 'Down' passenger. Truro West signal-box is in the yard.

Maurice Dart collection

7400 class 0–6–0PT 7422, a local engine at the time, on shed pilot duties at Truro on 12.6.56. Another Truro engine, 9400 class 0–6–0PT 8486 is on a Falmouth branch train in the station.

Denis Richards

Truro shed yard on 16.2.58 with permanent way work in progress. Locos visible are 'Grange' class 4–6–0 6805 *Broughton Grange* and 'Hall' class 4–6–0 6931 *Aldborough Hall*, both shedded at Truro with, in the background, 4300 class 2–6–0 6300 of St Blazey shed.

At times when either the Truro or Penzance turntable was out of action, a batch of large Prairie tanks was drafted in on loan to replace tender engines. On this occasion on 24.5.56 the Penzance table was under repair and Truro shed yard is host to 5101 class 4134 shedded at Carmarthen with Newton Abbot's 'County' class 4–6–0 1018 *County of Leicester* in the background. Spotters had a field day when this occurred as the big tanks came from a wide variety of sheds as far afield as Birkenhead.

Truro shed yard with 4575 class Prairie tank 5505 and 9400 0–6–0PT 8485, both at their home shed, on 21.5.57.

One of Truro's small Prairie tanks, 4500 class 4574 in light steam beyond the turntable on 21.5.57.

Truro's own 5101 class Prairie tank 4108 being coaled at the shed on 6.2.60; the system in use being unusual for an ex-GWR shed.

Just at the end of steam at Truro, a withdrawn 9400 class 0–6–0PT was sent down to act as a stationary boiler. 8408, seen here on 28.4.62, was quite a catch for local spotters, having been shedded at Danygraig and Swansea East Dock.

Larry Crosier

Truro shed supplied a Prairie tank for freight duties on the branch to Newham (goods), the ex West Cornwall Railway terminus. 4575 class 5537 is shunting the siding off the Newham branch into Truro Gas Works on 16.12.61. Closure took place on 17.11.71.

Larry Crosier

A pair of 8750 class 0–6–0PTs from Truro shed working a 'Down' Falmouth branch passenger crossing Carnon viaduct on 25.2.61. The locos are 4622 and 9635.

Michael Messenger

Inside the shed at Falmouth Docks on 17.4.63 are a pair of 0–4–0STs, No. 6 built by Pecketts (1530 of 1919) and No. 3 built by Hawthorn Leslie (3648 of 1926).

4575 class 2–6–2T 5500 of Truro shed backs the 9.51 a.m. from Truro out of Falmouth station to run around on 7.5.59.

Michael Mensing

Falmouth Docks No. 4, an 0–4–0ST built by Hawthorn Leslie in 1927, works No. 3670 on 17.4.63.

4575 class 2–6–2T 4587 of Truro shed at Shepherds with a Newquay–Truro via Chacewater train on 17.8.58. This route closed completely on 4.2.63.

Anthony Bennett

4500 class 2–6–2T 4566 of Penzance shed at Gwinear Road on 24.5.57 with the 7.00 p.m. from Helston. On 8.10.64 this branch closed completely and the station site was cleared.

A Penzance 2–6–2T of the 4575 class, 5545 shunts at Nancegollan goods yard on 16.12.61.
Larry Crosier

4575 class 2–6–2T 5545 of Penzance shed bursts through the narrow bridge past Truthall Halt with its typical GWR 'pagoda' shelter on 16.12.61.

Larry Crosier

Penzance-allocated 4575 class 2–6–2T 5508 at Helston with the 9.50 a.m. to Gwinear Road on 16.12.61. The goods shed is behind the loco and plenty of vans are in evidence.

Larry Crosier

A scene with a difference at Hayle wharves. A pair of horses shunting a wagon and a steam crane in the background, with plenty of wagons in the sidings beyond. This photograph probably dates from the late forties or early fifties. Horses were used here until 1961 and doubtless, on cold crisp days, their breath resembled steam. The branch down to the wharves, which was on a gradient of 1:30, closed in 1967 to general traffic and most sidings were removed by 1971.

Roger Winnen for the late D. Penhaul

A pair of Penzance-allocated 4500 class 2–6–2Ts at Lelant with a train from St Ives to St Erth on 14.7.61. The rear engine is 4566, the front one being 4549, with GWR-type buffer beam number and still retaining inside steam pipes.

Peter Gray

4500 class 2–6–2T 4570 of Penzance at St Erth with a train from St Ives on 17.8.58. There is plenty of traffic in the yard.

Anthony Bennett

4500 Class 2–6–2T 4564 was the last steam engine to stay overnight in St Ives shed, seen here the next morning leaving for the station on 9.9.61.

Peter Gray

A Penzance engine, 4500 2–6–2T 4547, being coaled on 16.2.58 at its home shed, situated at Long Rock, east of Ponsondane carriage sidings, approximately one mile from Penzance station.

Three locally-allocated 4500 class 2–6–2Ts lined up inside Penzance shed on the afternoon of 16.2.58. They are 4545, 4540 and 4563. The side of the cab visible on the right belongs to another Penzance engine, 'Grange' class 4–6–0 6800 *Arlington Grange*.

'Grange' class 4–6–0 6825 'Llanvair Grange' outside its home shed at Penzance on 16.2.58.

'Grange' class 4–6–0 6816 *Frankton Grange*, a Penzance engine, devoid of its tender, and bearing a GWR 'NOT TO BE MOVED' sign, stands outside the 'factory' at Long Rock shed on 16.2.58.

'Britannia' class Pacific 70019 *Lightning* shedded at Laira brings the 'Down' 'Cornish Riviera', known as 'The Limited' to countless railwaymen, into Penzance around 1952. Notice the water tank standing on the site of an early engine shed.

Maurice Dart collection (Brian A. Butt)

Plymouth Railway Circle and the RCTS ran a rail tour from Exeter St Davids to Penzance, called 'The Cornubian', as a farewell to steam in Devon and Cornwall. It was hauled between Exeter and Plymouth by 2884 class 2–8–0 2887 of Taunton shed and between Plymouth and Penzance by 'Westcountry' class Pacific 34002 *Salisbury* allocated to Exmouth junction shed. This was the one and only visit of this class to the ex-GWR main line in Cornwall on 3.5.64. The engine is seen at Penzance, backing on to the train after turning and being coaled and watered at Long Rock shed.

3440 *City of Truro* worked a special train of six coaches from Plymouth to Penzance on 15.9.57 and is seen after arrival at the westernmost outpost of the GWR.

Larry Crosier

2884 class 2–8–0 2886 has come off Laira shed via the Speedway curve and Lipson junction to turn. The crew enjoy the sun in the cab of this Banbury-allocated loco while awaiting the road past the back of Laira junction box in August 1951.

4400 class 2–6–2 4401 waits on the 'Up' relief line with a PW train at Laira junction while a spotter gazes at the valve gear in June 1953.

Two miles west of Penzance lies the village of Newlyn, on the west side of which is Penlee Quarry, which operated a 2 ft gauge railway down to the harbour. One of the steam locos survived, preserved on site, adorned with a television aerial after use in a local carnival procession. It was always described as an Orenstein and Koppel 0–4–0WT built around 1900, but also stated to be No. 73 constructed by Freud in 1901. It is seen here in a derelict state by the shore at Newlyn on 18.11.56. From 31.7.72 the railway was replaced with a conveyor belt and lorries.

LELANT